E V I D E N C E

Also by Luc Sante

LOW LIFE

EVIDENCE · LUC SANTE

Farrar, Straus and Giroux · New York

Library of Congress Cataloging-in-Publication Data
Sante, Luc.
Evidence / Luc Sante.—1st ed.
p.   cm.
1. Crime—New York (N.Y.)—History—20th century.   2. Crime—New York (N.Y.)—History—20th century—Pictorial works.   3. Legal photography—New York (N.Y.)—History—20th century.   I. Title.
HV6795..N5S26   1992   364.1'09747'109041—dc20   92-11263 CIP

All photographs courtesy of the Municipal Archives, Department of Records and Information Services, City of New York

I would like to express my thanks, first and foremost, to Kenneth Cobb, Evelyn Gonzales, and the rest of the staff at the Municipal Archives, as well as to John R. Podracky and Sergeant Romano of the Police Academy Museum, Dr. Mark L. Taff of the New York Society of Forensic Sciences, and the staffs of the New York Public Library Main Branch (especially the long-suffering microforms desk), the Schomberg Center for Research in Black Culture, the Municipal Reference Library, and the library of the John Jay College of Criminal Justice. Big thanks, too, to David Higginbotham for teaching me about cameras, and above all to M.H.P., who like a medium drew this text out of me.

To Melissa Pierson

CONTENTS

Time in its passing casts off particles of itself in the form of images, documents, relics, junk. Nobody can seize time once it is gone, so we must make do with such husks, the ones that have not yet succeeded in disintegrating. These forms repose in cardboard boxes and closets, in old houses and attics, in filing cabinets and mini-storage warehouses, in museums and libraries, in archives. In a great city such as New York there are collections of artifacts and boneyards of information everywhere. Among these are dissertations that will never be read, codes that will never be deciphered, objects whose particular import will never be understood, and the traces of innumerable human beings lost to history once and for all, without monuments or descendants or living memory, just a name somewhere in an official record consulted rarely if at all.

The Municipal Archives, which occupies a lower corner of the impressive old Beaux-Arts Surrogate's Court building at Chambers and Centre streets, contains birth and death and marriage records, the files of former mayors and district attorneys, the leavings of city commissions and departments. It is a cool place, well lit, not musty. Every day a scattering of historical researchers and a larger number of genealogists sit at the microfilm readers dowsing their way through copies of, say, the 1895 Police Census, looking for a faint footprint that may have been left there by someone who cannot be recalled in any other fashion. I went there while I was working on my book *Low Life*, not looking for any specific or exact documents, just for clues to what things were like in the city's slum and vice districts a hundred or so years ago. I didn't know what the archives possessed, exactly, and I was pursuing the non-method I used for that research, which consisted of trusting in a certain magnetic charge—I would know what I was looking for when I saw it—and then passing streams of miscellaneous data in review. In that spirit I worked my way fruitlessly through the microfilmed photographic collection of the Department of Docks and Wharves (most of the pictures obliterated by moisture, acidity, or general decay), the endless negative copies of precinct blotters in spidery copperplate script, interminably recording drunk-and-disorderly charges against forgotten persons on forgotten nights, and sundry other files of, to me, intangible interest.

It was, I think, on my third visit that Kenneth Cobb, the director of the archives, wondered if I'd be interested in seeing the Police Department photo collection. I gulped and said yes, and presently a library cart was wheeled out from a back room, laden with fifteen fat ring binders in archival boxes. As soon as I pulled out the first volume and began leafing through the pages of prints, my eyes widened. Nothing in the reams of photographic documentation I'd sorted through—countless inert pictures of buildings, posed ranks of functionaries, fuzzy views of empty streets devoid of detail—had prepared me for this. Here was a true record of the texture and grain of a lost New York, laid bare by the circumstances of murder. Lives stopped by razor or bullet were frozen by a flash of powder, the lens according these lives their properties—their petticoats and button shoes and calendars and cuspidors and beer bottles and wallpaper. The pictures were not just detailed documents, either,

but astonishing works in their medium. I thought I had come across the traces of a forgotten master, who seemed to prefigure the pitiless flashlit realism of Weegee while having affinities to Eugène Atget's passionate documentary lyricism. A style seemed to announce itself, deliberate and inimitable.

Confusingly, the photographs in the albums were organized by no principle that I could detect. The pictures that made me gasp were intermittent, shuffled together with copies of chauffeurs' licenses and out-of-town Bertillon records (painstaking lists of criminals' body measurements, according to a now obsolete identification method) and magnified views of pieces of jewelry and barely decipherable snapshots. In addition, there were lengthy and boring series of intradepartmental subjects: police dogs, for example, or horses, or studies of urinals at different station houses. There was a copy of a Black Hand threat letter, decorated with obscene drawings, and even an enigmatic set of shots, from various angles, of a man's right hand with two thumbs. I was no more enlightened by the captions, which comprised the fifteenth volume. I discovered, first of all, that although there were 1,400 images in the collection, considerably fewer were actually represented by prints. The negatives were glass plates, and many had cracked or been ruinously chipped, or their emulsion had stuck to the envelopes in which they had been stored. Furthermore, the captions were erratic. A minority were original to the photographs, transcribed from the discarded envelopes; the others, compensating for missing or illegible labels, represented guesses or skeletal descriptions by the archivists. Thus, a truly enigmatic image would yield up no more information than "Homicide victim male interior." The most I was able to ascertain was that the pictures dated from between 1914 and 1918 (with a few mug shots from the 1920s mixed in and two photos of a vacant lot bearing a crop of marijuana that dated from 1935). The collection appeared to be a slice of the New York Police Department's documentation that had been extracted, shaken up, and then dropped. I was puzzled as well as stirred, but for my purposes at the time I was satisfied with choosing a few appropriate pictures and having them copied.

But the pictures would not leave me alone. I found that I thought about them frequently, able to recall this or that image in disconcerting detail. I went back a number of times to look at the collection and, finally, plunged into the task of investigating their context and the circumstances of their making. All the while, their mystery increased. Problems and questions appeared in every direction, and each individual picture wove its own tangle. Why had they been taken? Who took them? What sort of truth were they supposed to represent? How did they come to have such a singular look about them? Why had they been preserved, and then neglected, and then preserved again? Why just those five years? What could account for the alternation of horror and emptiness in their depictions? On the horizon loomed some of the most perplexing knots raised by photography, raised anew by these examples: about truth, and transparency, and intrusion, and power, and individual style, and permanence.

I will attempt to address those questions in the following pages, but one of them, at least, can be given its sadly banal answer. It seems that in 1983 or '84, when the city was in the process of cleaning out the old police headquarters on Centre Street as a condition of its sale to private interests, workers removed roomfuls of files from its innards, and those files were dumped into the East River. (This was scarcely unprecedented; a forensic historian, writing in 1961, noted that "a few years ago," the NYPD, needing filing space, had taken thousands of its nineteenth-century glass-plate mug shots and likewise consigned them to New York Bay.) The city's archivists were informed too late, but, according to John R. Podracky, then of the Municipal Archives and now curator of the Police Academy Museum, they got there in time to find a small room under a staircase that had been overlooked by the workers. It contained filing cabinets that held those 1,400 plates, housed in manila envelopes, neglected for nearly three-quarters of a century and allowed to deteriorate. All the earlier New York Police Department work in forensic photography, most of the information concerning the surviving pictures, and probably a good deal of the later work as well (the NYPD, citing legal fears, is loath to discuss its archival holdings with outsiders), is lost forever.

The photographs on the following pages may inspire horror, as well as pity, and maybe morbid fascination and dull voyeurism. This is unavoidable, but it is not intended. I am presenting them because of their terrible eloquence and their nagging silence. I cannot mitigate the act of disrespect that is implicit in the act of looking at them, but their power is too strong to ignore; they demand confrontation as death demands it. I offer this work as a memorial to these dead, named and anonymous, as well as to their now equally dead photographers: John Golden, Clement Christensen, Arthur DeVoe, Frederick Zwirz, Charles Abrams, Charles Carsbrer, and perhaps unrecorded others.

L.S.

EVIDENCE

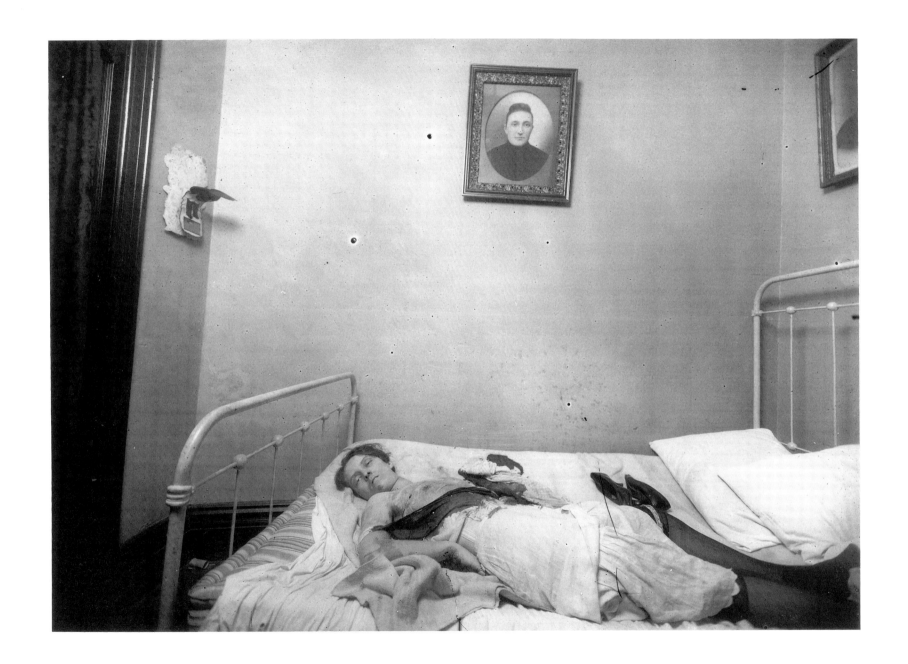

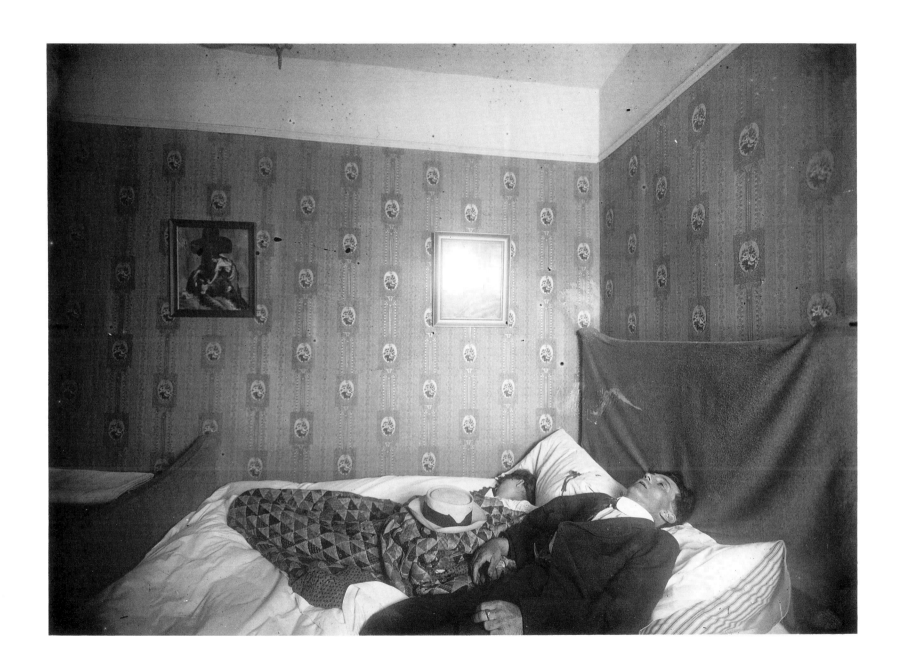

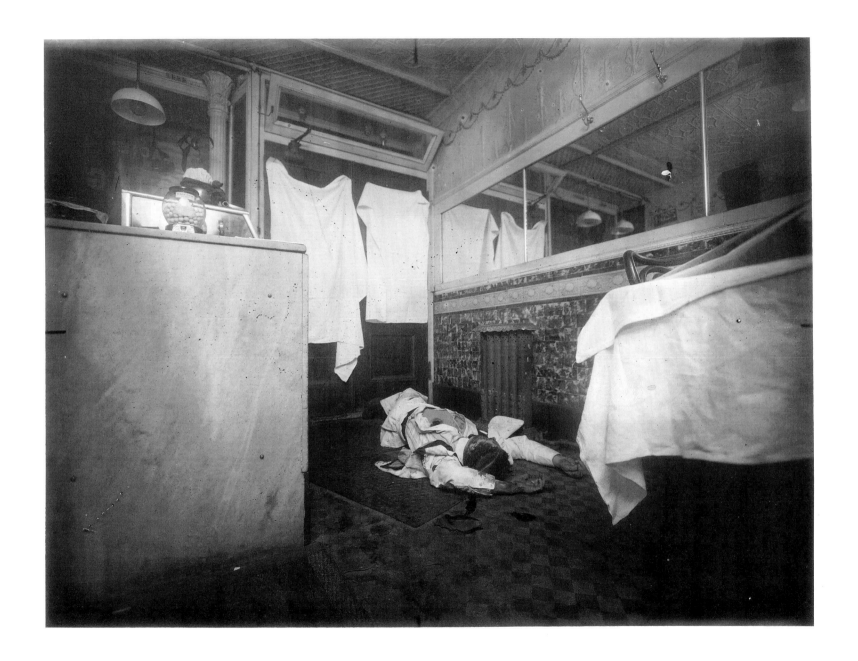

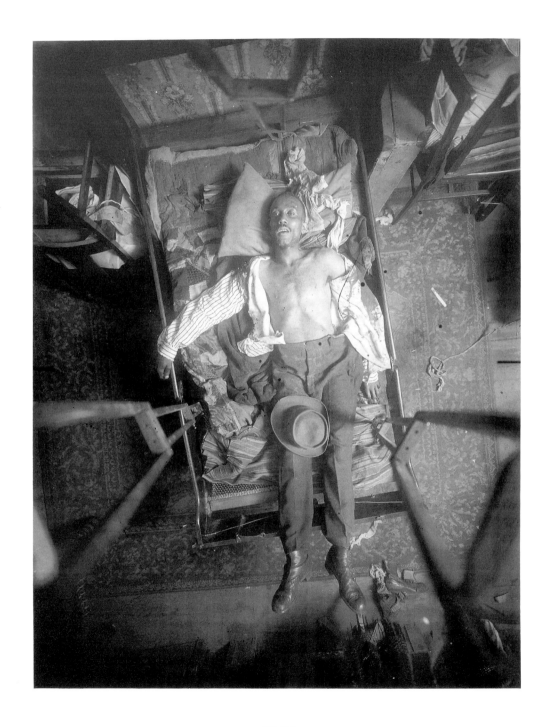

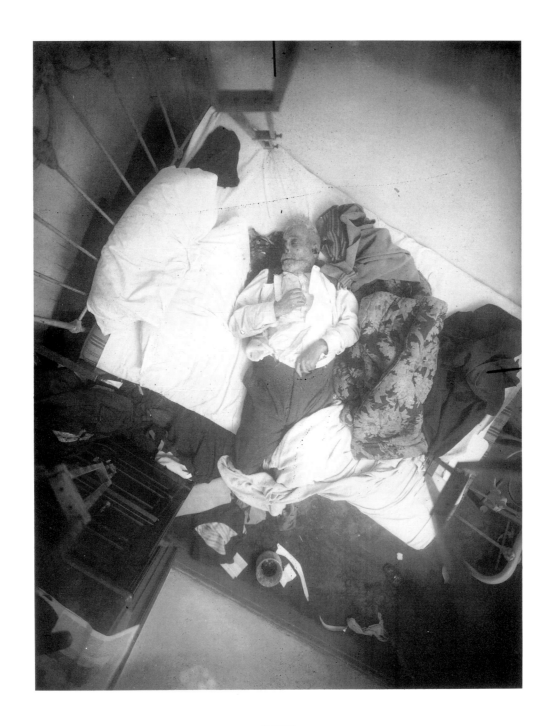

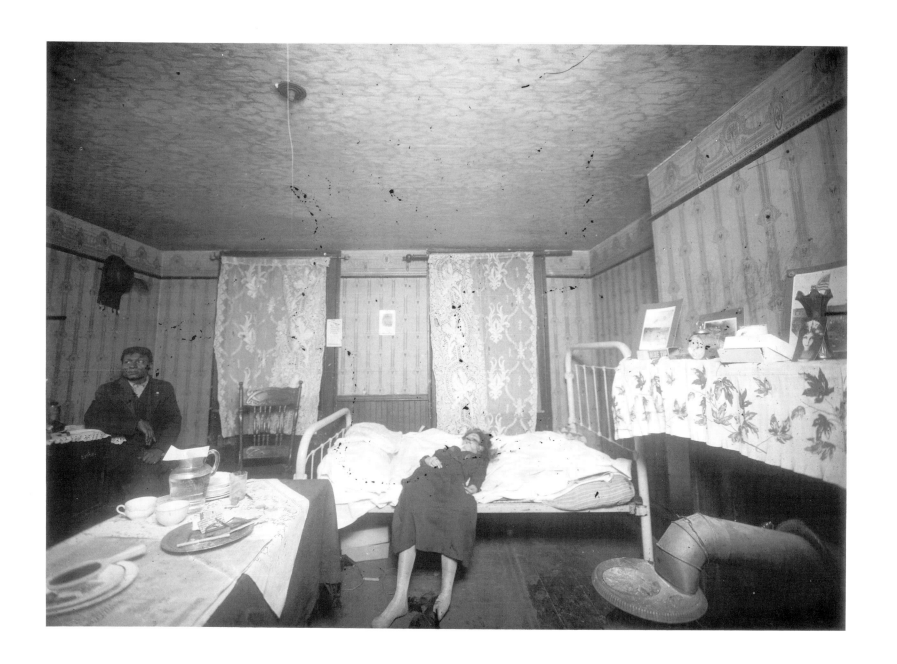

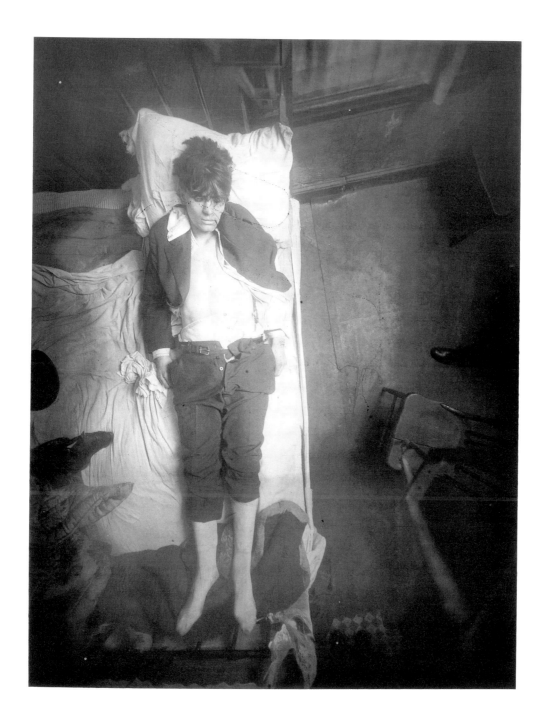

Police-blotter time consists of a long night and a short day. It is time that slips out of normal reckoning. Proclamations are made during the business day; everybody knows where they were when the bomb went off. Obscure homicides, however, take place in what seems like an extra pocket of the temporal continuum, in some unregulated patch between hours. The locations, meanwhile, define banality: bedrooms, bars, back streets, alleys, vacant lots, storerooms, hovels, hallways. A prosaic life, conducted in such open ordinariness that it might as well be a cloak of secrecy, is lit up all at once, at its termination. You do not have to be glamorous to meet a violent end; it can happen any old way—by mistake, for failing to give somebody a cigarette, for loving too much or too little, for wearing the wrong hat. Suddenly that supine figure, beneath notice when erect an hour ago, becomes an object of interest, at least momentarily. An alarm is given; the cops rush in; evidence is sought. A police photographer records the scene, in the process uniting, for the last time and in ways that go beyond forensic significance, the body and its familiars.

These pictures, taken so long ago that the people in them would now be dead even if they had enjoyed long and untroubled lives, exist in an eternal present that preserves their subjects between extinction and decay. The ones without bodies in them—nearly all of these are uncaptioned, their significance lost—are just as ominous, even viewed separately. Taken together, they become stills from a film, a nightmare ride from room to room in the small hours: the working day of a professional witness or a fingerprinter of corpses, perhaps, but without the protective cynicism of such a trade, more like a dream spent hurtling around trying to keep appointments, but the parties keep turning up dead. There is a mystery here which is only partly accounted for by the period clothes and the wide-angle lens and the flash powder. If photographs are supposed to freeze time, these crystallize what is already frozen, the aftermath of violence, like a voice-print of a scream. If photographs extend life, in memory and imagination, these extend death, not as a permanent condition the way tombstones do, but as a stage, an active moment of inactivity. Their subjects are constantly in the process of moving toward obliteration. It is death upon death, from animal to document.

We think we know how to look at death because we've looked at paintings: the dead Patroclus, the dead Ajax, the dead Christ, the dead Marat, dire tableaux of butchered limbs in baroque versions of antiquity. Photography allows less of a remove, but maybe it is possible to inure oneself to Alexander Gardner's Civil War battlefields full of corpses or the trophy or memorial images of propped-up dead Communards or Dalton Gang members. Those bodies become historical or symbolic, and their flesh is thus transsubstantiated mentally into some odorless and enduring substance like marble or wax. The pictures from concentration camps are unendurable, but anger and resolution can eclipse revulsion in the will if not in the craw. These photographs of quotidian death provoke a different response. Their triviality is no defense against them, rather the opposite, and if the datedness of their properties allows some distance, it is immediately can-

celed by the explosive light of the magnesium powder, which makes every detail stand out in relief, and the looming distortion of the wide-angle lens, which swallows the viewer in its hemispheric maw, along with the anamorphic warping of the tripod legs in the overhead shots, which imprison sight. In addition, these photographs lack the functions that are usually attached to images of death. They do not memorialize, or ennoble, or declare triumph, or cry for vengeance. As evidence, they are mere affectless records, concerned with details, as they themselves became details in the wider scope of police philosophy, which is far less concerned with the value of life than with the value of order. They are bookkeeping entries, with no transfiguring mission, and so serve death up raw and unmediated.

The dead in these pictures are in the room, not just their room but our room. They occupy the proscenium of their separate histories and their shared historical time, but insistently break loose from it, in part because of how the pictures were made, and in part because there is so little difference, really, between them and the victims of urban violence we mostly do not see on the streets around us but read about briefly in the newspapers and then think of statistically or metaphorically. In looking at these bodies, cold for three-quarters of a century, it is difficult to avoid a sense that we are violating them afresh, that we are breaking a taboo as old as the practice of shutting the eyes of cadavers and weighing down their lids. We barge into the room and pick things up with the insensitivity and gracelessness of a tabloid reporter stealing the only portrait of the deceased from his mother's bedside, or of a television journalist slapping the mother with pointless questions while she weeps on camera. We are caught knowing too much and too little at once, wanting to peer beyond the edges of the frame while feeling a reproach coming from somewhere past that margin, or that we are calling down a curse.

Maybe we intrude upon these dead by looking at them, but then they intrude upon us by virtue of being looked at. In *De Rerum Natura*, the Roman poet and philosopher Lucretius posited that "what we call 'images' of things" are "an outer skin or film" that is "perpetually peeled off the surface of objects and flying this way and that through the air . . . each wearing the aspect and form of the object from whose body it has emanated." This film has the capacity to "startle us with the notion that spirits may get loose from Hades and ghosts hover about among the living, and that some part of us may survive after death when body and mind alike have been disintegrated and dissolved into their component atoms." Primitive though this might be as physics, it is an apt evocation of the house of spooks that is photography, and in particular these pictures of the dead. Some of these bodies may never have been photographed in life; in death each has found a stance that seems perfected, and can detach itself from its background to float at will.

Photography is a medium; that is, an intermediate agency between the scene or object depicted and the eyes of the viewer. The word also carries a trace of one of its secondary meanings—a conduit between the living and the world of the spirits. As Roland Barthes, among others, has pointed out, every photograph is in some sense about death. We look at pictures from the past and know that everybody in them is now dead, although we do not always examine this knowledge. Even last month's snapshots present us with food that has been eaten, snow that has melted, joys that have faded, and circumstances that will never again be reproduced. Thus, every photograph is haunted, and, further, is the occasion of a haunting. These pictures multiply this factor, not least because in them can be seen reflected the lack of foreknowledge of their subjects, their presumption to life. Photography, like murder, interrupts life, as was understood by those proverbial savages—Balzac was one of them—who feared for their souls around the camera. But most photographs are charged with only a moment; these are custodians of entire existences, the summing-up before the grave.

The uninhabited pictures are pregnant with implication, again, partly as a consequence of lighting and lens. And there are incidental factors that influence the viewer but may or may not be germane to the deed associated with the site: shadows, stains, footprints in the snow. The stains may indeed be blood, the footprints may be those of the escaped murderer, or they may not be. Every detail of these pictures, relevant or not, has a weight, as if it had been chosen, and the compositions can seem impossibly definitive. The empty pictures may lack the unifying presence of death, but their power of suggestion derives from their preternatural stillness and their lack of an obvious referent, the deathlike void in their centers. Concerning Atget's photographs of Paris streets with few people and fewer activities, Walter Benjamin wrote:

Not for nothing were pictures of Atget compared with those of the scene of a crime. But is not every spot of our cities the scene of a crime? every passerby a perpetrator? Does not the photographer— descendant of augurers and haruspices—uncover guilt in his pictures?

The more empty the photograph, the more it will imply horror. There are several reasons for this. Cities, of course, breed crime, in thought as well as in deed, and this can extend to any site that bears the trace of human occupation (and Benjamin, as we shall see, was more literally correct than he intended in writing that the photographer uncovers guilt). In addition, we have come to accept certain kinds of photographs as pertaining to tragedy, or at least to legal evidence: the kind that show up reproduced in newsmagazines after a crime, empty or blurred, badly framed or wrenchingly banal. They are the pictures of the vacant house after the massacre, of the field in which the body was found, or the snapshots that constitute the only likeness of the victim or that prove that the murderer once passed for normal, just like any neighbor. Empty photographs have no reason to be except to show that which cannot be shown.

Furthermore, evidence is a magnet of the random. It is precisely those objects that inspire contempt, if we think of them at all in the course of daily usage, that are most likely to seem poignant when drawn into the circle of evidence by association. The enduring fascination with "true crime" in our culture (and the distinction is worth making, since in fictional crime the locations and objects are almost always overdetermined) depends only partly on shock or evil. The spectacle of ordinary things made immanent by proximity to violence is a routinely available surrealist event. The fact that every life is a chaos of incidentals ensures that sudden death will magnify disorder; any ridiculous moment might be the last moment, any insignificant object might be forever associated with you through some terminal juxtaposition. In such tangles can perhaps be found the deep origins of childhood fears: the admonition not to make faces, lest your features freeze in the grimace; the instruction to wear clean underwear "in case something happens"; the threat that God will judge you in accordance with whatever you are doing at the last moment of your life. In viewing these pictures, we are in the position of that God: those unfortunates who happened to get themselves murdered in a saloon we label as drunkards without even thinking about it; women sprawled on beds are likely to be taken for prostitutes.

The faces death makes are distortions, but they are likenesses of the forms that extremity takes: fatigue or fear or disbelief or something resembling exaltation, or, if one is lucky, sleep. The people in these pictures show us what we will look like, even if we die in bed of natural causes, and this is part of their threat to us, and part of the reason for our sense of a taboo. They are chronologically our elders, and our elders because they have gotten to that point before us, but our contemporaries because they are fixed forever at that point. In this way they are like the famous "bog people" of Denmark, preserved in cold mud for millennia, who are surprising because they are so "lifelike," because they are dead but not disintegrated, because although they are dead they display faces that seem to retain the ability to show emotion. The people in these pictures are fixed in their last emotion, slipping off toward rigor mortis, the final human activity before the microbes take over. This is an excruciatingly intimate sight, and perhaps it is the burden of this intimacy that makes the corpses in these pictures seem more real than the living cops or spectators who can be peripherally glimpsed. This is also why we want to turn away, shudder, recoil from the sight of death, even when it is not violent, even when it is so ordinary. The responsibility of witness that is thrust at us is too grave; when such a thing comes from a stranger, it is as if we had been entrusted with his or her existence. But if we turn away, aren't we in danger of denying that existence? The terrible gift that the dead make to the living is that of sight, which is to say foreknowledge; in return they demand memory, which is to say acknowledgment.

1. This picture has no surviving caption. There is no way of knowing in what year it was taken, but the election posters on the storefront set the time as, probably, late October or early November. The three-story building down the street announces itself as a factory of polishing and electroplating materials, and gives its address as 25 and 27 Jackson Street. This is most likely Jackson Street in Greenpoint, Brooklyn, near the border of Williamsburg. It is significant that this gun is the only weapon to be seen in these pictures—weapons were then immediately discharged and taken away for fingerprinting before any pictures were taken, whereas today photography would precede any alteration of the scene as found by police. It is difficult to make out the specifics of the gun, but it looks like a .38 revolver, perhaps a Colt "Police Positive." The elliptoid ring that resembles glare and in some of the other pictures might actually be mistaken

for a chalk circle is merely the effect of moisture on the emulsion of the glass negative. The small black line at the bottom of the frame (other pictures show four such, in the center of each arm of the frame) is the image of the wire cradle that held the plate in the camera. Policemen and maybe onlookers can be just barely made out down the street, next to a motor vehicle. None of the stains on the road surface means anything.

2. "19305 undersize." This caption refers to the file number and the size of the plate, which in this case would mean that it is smaller than 8 × 10. The number is puzzling in two ways. First, such numbers attached to other photographs in the series run consecutively up to roughly 2000; a five-digit number would either date it much later than the others, which seems unlikely, or else it incorporates a

subordinate last digit, as if it had been written 1930/5, which would set it in 1918. More perplexing is the fact that the number is shared with the following plate; the body might conceivably be the same, but the circumstances are decidedly not. The Italian neighborhood could be any one of three or four in Manhattan and an equal number in Brooklyn; if the former, the low house number indicates possibly Thompson Street. It is spring or fall. The killing might have been in connection with a robbery or an argument on the street, although the open door of the laundry at left, along with the cloth to the left of the body, suggests something beginning inside the store and spilling out. Perhaps it is the laundryman who is striding down the hallway of the tenement house toward the open door. The onlooker at right foreground is almost certainly a detective. The object protruding from the hat of the deceased might simply be the lining.

3

3. "19305 undersize." What connection might there be between this plate and the preceding one? The resemblance between the corpses, such as it can be made out, is little more than superficial: nearly all men at the time wore dark suits, white shirts, and pointed shoes. This body, however, is almost certainly in a vacant lot, or perhaps an untended yard: concrete verges toward vegetation, garbage is abundant, and there is a wooden stepladder in view, which may have been brought there by the police. The deceased may have been felled from behind by a blunt instrument. He is bleeding from the mouth, but there is no other sign of

4

violence evident on his person. The larger amount of blood is at some distance from the body, toward the top of the frame. He has evidently not been robbed; he retains his watch and chain. What might at first resemble an official document lying next to him is probably an open magazine. The rather alarming look of the tripod legs is, of course, due to distortion by the wide-angle lens, probably around 25 mm. The legs at upper left are those of the photographer or another detective. The victim is middle-aged and somewhat prosperous, but his left hand reveals him to have once been a manual laborer.

4. "Homicide body of John Rogers 88 W. 134th St. Christensen 10/21/15 883." In spite of this very complete caption, the case proved untraceable. In large part, that is because the victim was black, and white newspapers recorded the misfortunes of black people only in exceptionally rare circumstances. Three black newspapers were published in New York during this time, but copies from the period have survived for only one of those, the *New York Age*, which printed sermons and social notes but seldom covered crime stories. The manner in which Rogers met death is impossible to say. There might be blood on the steps and near his head, but the stains might also be dirt. Rogers has apparently been partly undressed and examined, by cops or coroners, and then his jacket draped shut by the same parties. He looks respectable, but a glance at his trousers is enough to show that he was far from prosperous. He is lying in the front hallway of a small apartment building, which looks well maintained (it no longer stands, the site falling roughly in the center of Lenox Terrace Plaza).

5. No caption. It is winter, but his neckwear seems too flimsy to be a muffler; it may be ceremonial. There is no blood nor any indication of how he died. He is lying in a tenement hallway, which is fitted with the universal cheap wainscotting of the time, and a linoleum pattern that looks familiar from tenements today.

6. No caption. The archivists guessed that the location might be a political club, but the size of the room, the bunting, and the arrangement of chairs might just as easily belong to a meeting hall for the Odd Fellows, the Knights of Pythias, or the Ancient Order of Foresters, lodges of which, among hundreds of other fraternal organizations, abounded at the time. The trash and scuff marks suggest the aftermath of a function, which might indeed have been held not by the regular tenants of the hall but by one of any number of gangster-connected associations which specialized in "rackets," balls organized for the purpose of making profits on ticket sales and the rake-off from the bar. An overhead view of the victim shows more clearly that he has a rag tied around his head, that he has been partly undressed, and that he bears a small, neat bullet hole about two inches under his right nipple. The rag seems inexplicable, suggesting toothache at most, although I was informed by Dr. Mark Taff, of the New York Society of Forensic Sciences, that "wrapping is placed around the jaw to avoid facial

distortion from rigor mortis," which could be significant if the police intended to rely on photographs to identify the body. The victim is no more than twenty-five years old, looks Irish, and wears cheap, heavy side-button shoes.

5

7. "The Panther Boys three men shot (no homicide). Injured were John Russell, Jerome Geigerman, and George Cisneros (Det. Carmody & Mahoney, 3rd Br. on case) 942 Golden." The location appears to be a venue similar to the preceding scene's. It is probably not by design that the photographer focused on the floorboards and the chair and piano stool to the right to the exclusion of the rest of the room, but this probable accident gives the photograph an unwarranted air of mystery. In fact, the case in question here is probably the closest to an open-and-shut one among all these pictures. It appears to be a simple intragang brawl. The men seated at left are the presumed gang members (a few of them trying to conceal their identities), while the standing figures and possibly the men at right are cops. The seated forms all the way in the rear might be the injured parties. Of these, Russell and Cisneros dissolve into history, but Geigerman had enough of a subsequent career that his name turned up twice in *The New York Times*: once in 1918, when he was picked up as a member of an auto theft ring (which may have moved more than five hundred cars a year, not a small number for the time), and again in 1925, when he was held as part of a gang of rum-runners. From the file number, the case illustrated here can be dated approximately early December 1915. It seems anomalous

6

7

among a dossier devoted almost entirely to homicides, and the photograph appears strikingly lacking in purpose, but the reasons are lost to us.

8

8. No caption. She has bled very heavily; the spot above her right breast and the line extending away from it in both directions probably indicate a knife wound. The shoes on the bed and the relative lack of blood on the covers suggest that she was moved to the bed some time after the attack took place. From the number of such dispositions of bodies among the pictures here it might be reasonable to guess that victims were moved onto beds when they were still alive, and were photographed after they subsequently died. Here it is impossible to tell whether sexual assault took place as well as murder. The undressing, again, may have been the work of cops or physicians.

9

9. "Double homicide #708 6/17/15." Here, the two bodies, the lack of a weapon, and the clear indication that at least one of the parties died in bed (the bloodied pillowcase) throw conflicting signals at the viewer. It might be a crime of passion, or it might be an anachronistic gangland-style execution. The missing weapon proves a red herring, however, as the date points the way to newspaper accounts, among which the following seems definitive:

WIFE SLAIN BY A SUITOR NONE KNEW
MAN WHO KILLED MRS. CORNELIUS AND HIMSELF
NOT BURGLAR, AS AT FIRST THOUGHT,
BUT ADMIRER IDENTIFIED AS GEORGE F. MCAGHON,
OF THE PENNSYLVANIA RAILROAD,
HE LEAVES FOUR YOUNG CHILDREN.
CLIMBS INTO BROOKLYN HOME OF HIS VICTIM
THROUGH A WINDOW
MYSTERY IS STILL DEEP IN CASE

George McAghon, an assistant yardmaster of the Pennsylvania Railroad, was the man who killed Mrs. Barbara Cornelius, a 24-year-old bride, in the bedroom of her apartment at No. 90 Hopkinson Avenue, Brooklyn.

The husband, Carman Cornelius, rushed from the room calling for help when he was awakened by McAghon, whom he thought was a burglar. He had never seen the man before.

Evidence of Mrs. Cornelius's love affair was found in love notes on the backs of picture postcards hidden among feminine keepsakes in a trunk. They were signed only "G." They carried no postmark, but had been mailed in an envelope addressed to "Bessie."

Acting Captain Duane and Lieutenant McKirdy accepted McAghon's signet ring as proof of his identity. Coroner Frank Senior and Coroner's Physician Dr. Charles Wuest determined that there were two pistol wounds in Mrs. Cornelius's temple and one in McAghon's head. McAghon's hand bore a powder smudge.

One shot, aimed at the fleeing husband, was found buried in the wall opposite the window through which McAghon entered.

Carman Cornelius is connected with a produce house in one of the Brooklyn markets. Not strong physically, he has been home several days recovering from an illness. He usually leaves for work at one o'clock A.M., but was home on account of his health. McAghon entered about 1:30 A.M.

It was his second marriage. The dead woman, nee Barbara Seilein, was named as co-respondent in his divorce case. McAghon was never seen in the neighborhood, but Mrs. Cornelius had often used the pay telephone in a drugstore two blocks away at Decatur and Hopkinson Streets.

McAghon was required to carry a gun at his job. He was 35 years old and lived at No. 160 Erie Street, Jersey City. He had been an assistant foreman at the Harsimus Cove yard of the Pennsylvania Railroad for two years, at $120 monthly.

He was said to have had temperate habits, and attended St. Mary's Catholic Church. His wife had been dead two years, and his home was kept by his sister, Jennie McAghon. He leaves four children: Elizabeth, 12 years old, Margaret, 10 years, Mary, 7 years, and Jimmie, 5 years.

Identification of McAghon was made fourteen hours after the arrival of the police by William J. Morris of the Pennsylvania Railroad. Captain Duane of the Seventh Branch Bureau had traced the place where the dead man's clothing had been purchased to a store in Jersey City.

The window was only five feet from the pavement, and was open except for a wire screen. While climbing in McAghon was in full glare of several street lamps.

McAghon had been reported as a burglar in yesterday's late edition.

[Abridged from the *New York American*, June 18, 1915]

Despite the slender clue represented by the date, this tangled tale seems persuasive as an explanation for the scene in the photograph. In the picture frame in the center, bright with the glare of the magnesium powder,

can be seen the reflection of the door, immediately to the right of the bed, through which Cornelius fled. McAghon's signet ring is visible on his left middle finger. We seem to be in possession of most of the facts, but we have no idea why the murder-suicide took place. Was it premeditated, or was it a reaction to the husband's presence? Was Barbara Cornelius as treacherous as her prior career as a co-respondent is pointedly meant to suggest? Was the husband exactly as weak and as unknowing as the husbands in farces? We can wonder, too, about the scheduling of the trysts, which for McAghon must have involved a very long journey that included two ferry crossings and a lengthy streetcar ride all the way to Bedford-Stuyvesant. Of course, crimes of passion are proverbially the easiest to solve, and the most enduringly mysterious.

10. No caption, although another photograph in the archive of the same location is identified as being of the Café Roma. There was probably more than one establishment at the time bearing that name, so it is impossible to know whether this is the same Café Roma that stood at 169 Mulberry Street and which in September 1915 saw a brawl that left one man dead and another dying of both knife and bullet wounds. None of the parties in that incident, however, was a waiter, which the deceased in this photograph appears to be. It cannot be determined whether he was stabbed or shot. The cloths over the door panels are there to keep out both light and onlookers. There is no evident disarrangement of furniture. The motive may have been robbery.

11. No caption. There is so much blood present that it is impossible to say where it came from or by what means. The bartender may have been shot in the head, in the left side hidden by the tripod leg. The blood on his forearms may indicate that he put up a struggle. The cap at his feet may have been his own, or his assailant's.

12. "Homicide (female) 1917 (undersize) #1724 6/24/17." This mysterious picture, in its wet light, looks like a still from an early movie serial, although there is too much blood or dirt on the victim's face. The date suggests that it may represent the aftermath of the following incident:

GIRL SLAIN, MAN SHOT IN JOY RIDE
CABARET SINGER IS KILLED WHEN THREE 'FRIENDLY' STRANGERS ATTACK HER SWEETHEART

They were out for a good time in a big limousine—three young men and two girls. After a laughing tour of three cabarets it seemed perfectly natural to invite for a ride three men vaguely remembered by Allan Thompson of No. 503 West 105th Street, the driver of the car, as acquaintances.

Under the joyous white lights they piled in—Helen Wheelan, 17 years old, of No. 165 East 127th Street; Kitty Naughton, 23 years old, of No. 309 West 141st Street; Frank Devlin, of No. 140 West 103rd Street; Walter J. Brennan, of No. 309 West 141st Street; Thompson and the newcomers—and were off for the cool night roads of early yesterday morning.

The three strangers, one of whom, police say, is an ex-convict,

waited for a lonely spot in the Bronx. Then one made an insulting remark to Miss Wheelan. Devlin, her sweetheart, demanded an explanation.

"We'll have this out right here," retorted the stranger. The automobile stopped at 134th Street and Willow Avenue and the party got out.

Suddenly, according to police accounts, all three of the strange men attacked Devlin. Devlin went down; a revolver flashed and two shots went through the struggling man's spine; three more shots struck Miss Wheelan, killing her instantly.

Devlin was rushed to Lincoln Hospital, where he is said to be in danger of death. He told Coroner Healy he would not die before avenging his sweetheart's death. The other two men are held on $5000 bail as witnesses.

Four more arrests followed the discovery of the bullet-marked machine in a nearby garage last night. Harold Butler, of No. 165 West 128th Street; Julia Touhey, Miss Naughton's 18-year-old cousin, of No. 161 West 66th Street; and Theodore Kialy, of No. 56 West 100th Street, were locked up as witnesses.

Miss Wheelan, the murdered girl, was employed in a Broadway cabaret. Devlin, a private detective, had been attentive to her for several months.

[*New York American*, June 25, 1917]

This period story, with such refinements of detail as the occupations of the two victims, seems to have fired up the *American*'s rewrite man, so that he cast it as cheap fiction. It is not so much that the men in the story have no ages as that the women's are dangled as titillation.

The *Times* got there first with the story, reporting it the previous day, although its account is flatter and reports the dead woman's name, initially, as Nellie Weilman. This was corrected in the follow-up accounts, which revealed that Thompson was the chauffeur for one Harry Bergman, a real estate dealer of West 94th Street, whose car it was (might Thompson's claiming an address in the middle of the Hudson River have been an attempt to conceal himself?), that Wheelan was killed shielding Devlin with her body, and that the shots were thought to have been fired by Harold Butler. Eventually Michael J. Negliano, of East 118th Street, a process server by trade, confessed. Negliano claimed that Devlin had attacked Butler and then himself. "Negliano thought he was firing in self-defense, because Devlin had been telling Miss Wheelan to 'show him the gun.' " Although the location in the photograph accords with contemporary map features for the vicinity of 134th Street and Willow Avenue in the Bronx (there is still a railroad overpass there, and at the time there was also a ground-level trunk line), it may be difficult to accept the supine figure as having been a seventeen-year-old cabaret singer, and this can only be countered by pointing to changes in fashions, as well as, possibly, bloating.

13. "555 6th Bklyn suicide w/ her 3 children (gas) 10/15/15 by Z #870." This sad picture is matched by an equally sad and simple story:

FOUR DIE FROM GAS

Peter Connell, of No. 476 Sixth Avenue, Brooklyn, went yesterday to the home of his sister, Mrs. Josephine Huntsinger, at No. 555 Sixth Avenue, Brooklyn, to arrange for the funeral of his brother-in-law. The brother-in-law was drowned Monday.

Gas billowed from the flat. Connell dashed within. In the bedroom  *were the dead bodies of Mrs. Huntsinger and her three children— Alice, 13 years old; Elizabeth, 8 years old; and Emma, 3 years old.*

The five will be buried together.

[*New York American*, October 16, 1915]

14. No caption. A calendar dates the scene as June 1917. There is no sign of struggle in this meticulously ordered room, and the only possible indication of violence is the dull stain to the right of the body, which may or may not be blood. Once again, the undressing is undoubtedly the work of police or doctors, but if the victim had been white 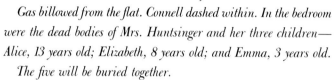 the responsible parties would unquestionably have tucked his penis back into his pants. There is a definite distension of the stomach that looks distinctly different from mere fat. Maybe poison was the cause.

15. "Homicide Roshinsky taken Chas. Abrams #1033 518 Fourth Avenue Astoria 2/15/16." This is another case in which, in spite of a thorough caption, the trail leads nowhere. The scene possesses an unearthly stillness that is immediately belied by the victim's right hand, which might be bloody or burned, and by the disarranged furniture.  This latter aspect is puzzling: the small table is tipped over far from the body, and although both it and the mirror chest (which is on casters) are obviously out of their accustomed positions, there is no indication of where those two pieces might go. The chest could fit only in some part of the room behind the photographer, and it could not have been wheeled past the recumbent Ms. Roshinsky. These might, therefore, be signs of a struggle. If it were not for these details, and the presence of the word "homicide" in the caption, one might be inclined to guess that the case was one of electrocution. There are headphones next to the body, and what might be a telegraph set just beyond it, along with an unnamable piece of equipment stuck beneath the small table along with what might be a carpet sweeper. What telegraph equipment might have been doing in a private apartment is anybody's guess. The place is well furnished, but evidently minuscule, although the bed appears to have been rolled forward. In its normal position there might be sufficient room to open the davenport.

16.

16. No caption, although it might be paired with the equally uncaptioned number 25. This hallway, on the ground floor of a tenement, might lead to a yard or to a rear building. That is probably blood on the floor, suggesting a victim who dragged him or herself into the body of the building after the assault.

17. "Homicide 2/14/18." The archivists unaccountably guessed that the victim here might be a sailor. Perhaps the shoes, or the trunk, or the calendar girls suggested it. In any event, the figure is quite evidently female, and not nearly as decayed as the poor condition of the plate might cause one to believe. The newspaper account clears up the more immediate mysteries:

WOMAN FOUND CRUELLY SLAIN IN OWN HOME
MRS. HELEN HAMMELL DEAD 24 HOURS WHEN DISCOVERED IN THE LODGING HOUSE SHE HAD RUN
MARKS OF SMALL TEETH AND BANDAGE ON WOUND POINT TO MEMBER OF OWN SEX AS ASSASSIN

Two pet dogs and a taciturn green parrot were the only witnesses to the murder of Mrs. Helen Hammell. She was slain in the lodging house she conducted at No. 507 West 23rd Street sometime on Wednesday. The body was discovered yesterday.

Mrs. Hammell's assailant obviously repented after the victim had been stunned by a blow on the back of the head. The wound was carefully bandaged, and a cloth found knotted around Mrs. Hammell's throat may have been placed there to stop the flow of blood rather than to strangle her.

A man's first instinct is escape, not to remain and play Good Samaritan.

In the next room, jewelry was found at more than $1000 worth, diamonds, and $860 in cash. The body was found on a couch in a rear bedroom in the basement.

Edward Kelly, who runs a pool room next door, heard screams at around noon on Wednesday. One lodger, who was home sleeping, heard Mrs. Hammell arguing with a woman.

Mrs. Hammell's husband works at Sailors' Snug Harbor and is only home on weekends.

A small piece of broomstick and a two-inch steel file are believed to be the weapons.

One of the most mystifying features of the case is that, despite the fact that the body was discovered on a couch in a rear bedroom, there is a wide blotch of blood on the door opening from the basement into the street. On the walls of the hall leading from this door to the bedroom are also bloodstains.

[Abridged from the *New York American*, February 15, 1918]

The blood might have been on the assailant's hands from contact with Hammell, and she or he might have been attempting to wipe it off before going out into the street. The assailant may, indeed, have been unaware that Hammell was dead or dying. What the account fails to say is how the two-inch steel file could have come into play; a small piece of broomstick, for that matter, hardly seems like a weapon that could deliver a fatal blow to the back of the head.

18 and **19.** "Photo of dead body of Marion who was murdered in shanty at Old Stone Rd & Bullshead Golden 1915." The newspapers next to her body supply the date of her demise: during the World Series, when the Red Sox beat the Phillies. Although she was a *Times* reader, that paper did not carry the story of her murder.

WOMAN MISER SLAIN; TWO BOARDERS HELD
With her throat cut from ear to ear, and a carving knife by her side, Marion Hart, 39 years old, was found dead in her lonely cottage,

No. 1093 Old Stone Road, Bull's Head, Staten Island, last night.

Calvin Decker, 39 years old, an oysterman, who boarded with her, found the body.

Decker and Julia Watson, 29 years old, who also boarded with the dead woman, were locked up.

Before she took Decker and Miss Watson as boarders the dead woman lived alone for some years and was regarded by the villagers as a hermit and a miser.

[*New York American*, October 14, 1915]

The *New York Evening Mail* of the same date stated that the house was Decker's, that Hart had been his housekeeper, that she was thirty-eight years old, and that she had been slain with an ax. There is, of course, no weapon to be seen in the picture. If we are looking at one half of the house, rather than a mere room within it, it would seen a bit small to take in a housekeeper, but maybe the term is used here as a euphemism for common-law wife. There is certainly a suggestion of a triangle, at least in the *American*'s presentation of the events. That Hart was considered a miser raises interesting possibilities. The media were fascinated by misers then, as they had been since the days of Hetty Green, the "witch of Wall Street," who was reputed to possess a fortune and yet saved tiny pieces of soap in an old stocking. Hart may have been thought a miser simply because she was educated enough to be a *Times* reader but lived in a shack. The newspaper refers to the epithet in the past tense in the body of the story, yet uses it in its headline, which might make the

20

reader believe that the killing had been over money. Such a motive is certainly not implausible, and if the killer had been an acquaintance there might not be any reason for the room to have been ransacked, but the question hangs. The dog, meanwhile, is frightened or docile, no more perturbed by the presence of the cops than, presumably, by the murder.

20. No caption. Another case in which the victim may have been assaulted before being removed to the uncomfortable-looking davenport on which he died. He looks young and undernourished, his waist half the size of that of his trousers. He is unshaven, which suggests either joblessness or an elapsed day between collapse and photography (beards, like fingernails, continue to grow after death). The blood would appear to be coming from his back.

21

21. No caption. He has been killed on a stair landing in a tenement house. He, too, seems to be bleeding from the back. This plate is in especially bad shape, with dirt, fingerprints, and a pronounced moisture ring. The effect of moisture also makes certain details, such as his right hand, appear almost solarized. He is probably Italian, probably a laborer, probably younger than his eyes look.

22

22. No caption. This person is perhaps male to judge by the hair, perhaps female to go by the hands. The stone covering the head may or may not have been the murder weapon. At first glance, the body might look like that of a

23

vagrant, but the coat is a good one and in fine condition, as can be seen by the hem of its skirt. There is no way to tell whether skirt or trousers are missing, or whether they have simply been pushed up below the coat. The bound hands, of course, make it a mystery. Was this a sex crime? part of a gang war? a kidnapping for ransom? The location is probably a park, rather than a mere lot, to judge by its wildness, so the body may have lain there for a considerable time before discovery.

23. No caption. The license plate is of 1918 issue. The story is almost certainly the following:

FIND BODY IN A BARREL
MURDERED MAN HAD THROAT CUT
AND 24 STAB WOUNDS

Three small children playing in a vacant lot in 45th Street, between Eighth and Ninth Streets [sic], in Brooklyn, at dusk yesterday came across a wine barrel the head of which had been covered by burlap nailed to the sides. They tore this off and saw a pair of feet sticking out. They ran away frightened and told a man, who notified the police of the Fourth Avenue Station. Captain Arthur Carey, Chief of the Homicide Bureau, took fingerprints and ordered the body removed to the Fourth Avenue Station.

There it was found the man had been murdered. His throat was cut, his face and forehead gashed, and there were 24 stab wounds on the upper part of his body. Identity was established by means of a draft card found in a pocket of the coat. This showed he was

The practice of stuffing bodies into barrels, usually with their tongues slit, is an old Mafia way of taking care of snitches. It was a habit associated with the New York City Mafia's first great capo, Ignazio Lupo, and was probably not ignored by the Brooklyn Camorra, either. In 1918 Lupo was in jail and many other old leaders were in the process of being forcibly retired, while the young bloods of the Unione Siciliana were waging a citywide leadership war. Candella may well have been a victim of this fray. The only other conceivable explanation would be a particularly demented crime of passion.

24. No caption. These are shotgun shacks of a sort that no longer exist in New York. The location may be Queens or Staten Island.

25. No caption. As previously mentioned, this picture is paired with number 16. The trail of blood which in that picture seemed to lead into the building from the hallway here might look as if it is headed out, from just outside the saloon. It is impossible to say at which end of the path the assault took place, or what happened to the body. The two men visible through the doorway are detectives.

26. No caption. The body is that of a black man, who is lying in the front hallway of a tenement. A crowd has gathered outside, in the rain, holding umbrellas. The cigarette butt on the floor might have been thrown there by anyone, including the cops.

27. No caption. Another tenement hallway victim, who has been shot or stabbed at a point probably between the collarbone and the heart. He is a strong man, a laborer, probably Jewish or Italian. The building is dingy, with cracks, hasty plastering, some kind of sub-graffiti chalk mark on the wall, and a common hallway sink.

28. No caption. The position of the young victim's coattail suggests that his pocket was picked after he fell. The location is a saloon, as can be seen from the brass rail and the spittoon at his feet. The official-looking document by his right arm is an announcement of the first annual ball of the McKinley Lodge No. 43 of the Knights of Pythias in Brooklyn, to be held November 3, 1917, admission 25 cents, and the other papers are additional copies of the same flier. Since the man was black, he was not invited, but probably was hired to post them.

29. No caption. This man, too, was killed in a bar, apparently shot in the chest. He has soiled himself at some point. His pockets are pulled out, which might be the work of the police, or of a pickpocket. The object poking out from under his pulled-back shirt on the left side of his body, which

29

30

31

32

33

might be a belt if it were in another spot, is unaccountable. A pack of Mecca cigarettes is somehow balanced on the footrail.

30. "Body Bessie Weils [sic] alias Dumont found in kitchen 5 Monroe St 4-2-17, undersized file #159 [last digit illegible] Charles E. Carsbrer." Here we have another detailed caption that leads nowhere. Her age is indeterminate, but her legs are in good shape. Her bare feet positioned by the bowl suggest that she might have been taking a footbath when the end came. She might, in fact, have been the victim of an accident rather than a homicide, pitching forward and cracking her skull, possibly not being found for a while. Her circumstances are manifestly poor, but the kitchen has sliding doors, an uncommon feature in tenements, which, being on Monroe Street, her home probably was. (It may have been on the notorious "Lung Block" and is now on the site of Knickerbocker Village.)

31. No caption. The male victim appears very well dressed, the female less so. That, together with the vast amount of blood she has shed compared to the apparently pristine condition of his body, suggests a murder-suicide, since suicides are noted, or were noted at the time, for their tendency to dress up before the act. The bed, curiously, has been disassembled, its hardware reposing against the wall at left, while the bedding may be represented by the pile that begins at extreme right. The embroidered or punctured cloth draped across the man's right leg is unidenti-

fiable. There is a trace of blood on the man's left hand, which might indicate a struggle. Despite the florid wallpaper, furnishings, and knickknacks, the room is in a tenement, albeit of a very well-kept sort.

32. No caption. She is on a dirt path in a park, clawing at the grass. It probably took her a while to die, and she may have taken off her cardigan in the process. The blood has soaked through her dress, but there is no suggestion of a wound there, it probably having been inflicted from the front.

33. No caption. She was pregnant. The tiles suggest a subway station.

34. No caption. This photograph seems utterly posed: there is no blood, and the positioning is altogether too neat. Again, a picture is given inadvertent mystery by technical uncertainty: the focus on the bulging foreground carpet roll puts the weight of the picture there, and the viewer half expects something to be concealed in it. Nothing else can be gleaned from this scene, which, unjustly in regard to its Middle Eastern subject, possibly a robbery victim, also has the air of a film serial about it.

35. No caption. This wasn't the 1915 case of the man who was killed in a pool hall by being pelted with billiard balls, but the flush of the man's face does point to possible hemorrhaging. The smear on the floor in the foreground may be a patch of blood. The object dangling from a string suspended from the ceiling at center is the cue-stick chalk, and the ominous object that also depends from the ceiling at left is, of course, the gas jet.

36. No caption. She has probably been stabbed or shot in the chest, and her right arm is blotched, although it does not seem to be cut. With peculiar symmetry, the topmost of the two pictures above her is a stock chromolithograph of the "dying mother" genre.

37. "Alberta Thomas (bl) 69 W 135 4/14/14 12:45 pm by Z murder 599."

MURDERS SWEETHEART;
SHOOTS AND CUTS HER

Miss Alberta Thomas, of 69 West 135th street, was murdered Tuesday morning between the hours of 9 and 10 o'clock by her sweetheart, Wilbur Willwood, who is said to be a railroad man. After Willwood had brutally cut and shot Miss Thomas he jumped out of the second story window, and was picked up in the court by persons living in the flat. His leg was broken, and he was taken to Harlem Hospital.

Jealousy is said to have prompted Willwood to murder his sweetheart. After shooting her four times the frenzied man took a razor which he used on his victim most industriously. When found the dead woman's face and body were badly cut.

Alberta Thomas roomed with a Mrs. Scott, who resides on the second floor, back, of 69 West 135th street. The couple were heard quarrelling shortly before the murder was committed. Willwood made a desperate effort to escape after he had killed his sweetheart, but broke his leg when he landed on the pavement in the court.

The injured man was held a prisoner and the police were summoned. When asked by the police how he had killed Miss Thomas, Willwood said, "I shot and cut her."

[*New York Age*, April 16, 1914]

Willwood's mad industry is evident. The room is apparently extremely small. The location is now on the site of Harlem Hospital.

38. No caption. The location of this scene is not evident, although the size of the table and the impersonal-looking prints may suggest a boardinghouse or a private drinking club, perhaps a blind tiger (a pre-Prohibition illegal bucketshop) of a relatively refined sort. The ceiling is low, which may mean that it is on an attic floor. The victim was probably shot from his right, since the larger hole in the window is probably the bullet's path of exit. The victim was well dressed, as his tie and his fancy fur hat indicate. Possibly, given the circumstances, he was a gangster.

39. "#1104 3/5/16 Pasquale Caruso shot and killed [illegible] Bertona body removed to home before I arrived. Photo also of Caruso taken at 170th Pct showing wounds on face, Golden." This exceedingly odd photograph belongs to a case that was well covered in the press.

39

40

41

42

43

VETERAN, 80, KILLS MAN, 64, WITH WAR GUN
AGED BROOKLYN RESIDENT SLAYS NEIGHBOR
AFTER BEING SLASHED IN FIGHT

With an army blunderbuss that he had carried in Italy's wars Pasquale Caruso, 80 years old, last night shot and killed Giuseppe Certona, 64 years old.

Caruso is a portrait painter and lives at No. 1402 66th Street, Brooklyn.

He was walking near his home when three sons of Certona threw snowballs at him. He walked in to their home, No. 1409 66th Street, to protest to their father. A bitter quarrel with Certona followed, and Certona is alleged to have slashed the aged man across the face with a knife.

Caruso hurried across the street to his own home, Certona following. Just inside the door was a blunderbuss. Caruso discharged it in Certona's face, killing him instantly. Then he fell fainting over the form of his victim.

The slayer hid in a cellar. Reserves from the Bath Beach station caught him. The aged artist admitted the killing, the police say. He is locked up in Brooklyn headquarters, charged with homicide.

[*New York American*, March 6, 1916]

The *Times* the same day headlined its story HIS CHAPLIN WALK CAUSE OF A MURDER. Apparently Caruso's rheumatism affected his gait, so that Certona's sons did not merely throw snowballs, they yelled, "Charlie Chaplin, Charlie Chaplin," and there was a whole mob of boys, not just Certona's. In any event, Caruso, described by the *Times* as a plasterer, blew off most of Certona's head with the gun with which he had fought under Garibaldi. Thus, this photograph, apparently so mysterious as a portrait of an erect corpse, must be a portrait of Caruso, the murderer. His eyes, on close inspection, prove to be open. The setting now reveals itself as unmistakably a police station, with its institutional bicolor paint job, its big desk, its fat electrical cord (the newspapers are being held up to concentrate the light).

40. "Nov 24 1915 #1032 2 bodies (male) elev shaft at 129 W 27 St." The fact that there are two bodies at the bottom of the shaft suggests something more than an accident, possibly a gang war byproduct. Nevertheless, the story did not make the papers. It is unclear whether the two died of injuries inflicted by means other than their fall. There is blood on the right-hand figure's shoulder; the other's hands are smeared with blood or grease or both. An unidentifiable object protrudes from under the left-hand man's vest. His posture suggests Adam, or a Romantic poet engaged in contemplation.

41. "Auto smashed into bldg 7th Ave & W 120 St." The car has managed to jump the curb and plow through the wrought-iron fence that usually separates an apartment-building moat like the one pictured from the pavement. In the process it has nearly dislodged one of the concrete parapets on the basement level, and perhaps knocked down three more slabs, widely spaced along the alley. The iron railing visible seems an unlikely frippery halfway up the windows at that height; perhaps it is the fence from the sidewalk side, rammed all the way across by the car's force. The driver may actually have gotten away with minimal injury. Note the primitive graffiti.

42. No caption. The scene is a tenement rooftop. The near-solarization on the disheveled man's face is, yet again, the effect of moisture on the plate, which, in addition, has apparently exaggerated the results of a daytime outdoor use of the flash. The man may have been the victim of an assault, illustrating the scene of the attack. The wide panel in the rear may be a billboard. The ominous silhouette at far left, which appears to be on wheels, is probably a detective.

43. "Park where Paul Richard 15 Lawn Ave was shot Christensen #529 1/17/16 file 966." The location is either Queens or Staten Island, both rather rural districts at the time. The snow is being whipped up by the wind, making it look like ambient grasses or tiny fireworks. There are probably too many footprints for those to be the point of the photograph. The figures in the background are cops.

44. No caption. The man appears to have been dead for some time and may have died of natural causes. There is dried blood in his ear, and he seems to be missing part of his nose. His room is no more than seven feet by ten. The jug at his feet is a cuspidor.

45. No caption. This skeletal figure, a worker in a grocery or a warehouse, has seemingly been the victim of multiple blows or stab wounds. Puzzlingly, his garb suggests pajamas, and he is either barefoot or in his stocking feet. In fact, the setting may not be a grocery back room at all but a stair landing in a particularly crude tenement, with a common hallway sink.

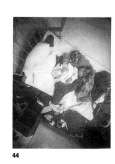
44

46. No caption. The New York Edison Company calendar in the rear may say 1919. She has blood on her face, apparently emanating from her nose, but there is no obvious sign of violence. The man at left, possibly her husband, does not look like the perpetrator. Dr. Taff, the forensic scientist I consulted, suggested that she may have been a suicide, in which case the letter on top of the pitcher might be her explanatory note, but it would be odd for a suicide to be sliding off the bed and to be half in and half out of her shoes. The viewer's eyes keep coming back to the newspaper clipping on the plate at near left, but it merely appears to be part of a *New York Tribune* editorial; if there is a salient clue, it would be on the reverse.

45

46

47. "Killed by William Burke at 140 W 32 on 1/22/16 DeVoe file #1002." The caption leads nowhere; the blood from the ear could mean any number of things. Much can be gleaned about the subject's life from this photograph, but little about his death.

47

48

49

50

51

48. No caption. The subject has been prepared for burial, bound and tagged. He may have been photographed as an afterthought; perhaps a seemingly natural death later proved to have more complicated sidelights. The head wrap is, once again, probably intended to facilitate identification via the photograph; the same may apply to what appears to be cotton stuffed in his mouth. Despite the preparation of the corpse, no attempt has been made to clean the blood, which seems to come from a stab wound near the thoracic cavity. The location, suggestive of both a medical examination chamber and a basement storeroom, may be a slap-up coroner's room in a police station, or a room in the morgue. The package wrapped in the *Times* near his head probably contains related evidentiary material; the tag is inscribed with a name and an age, neither of which is legible. Another such package is on the table at right. What looks like blood near the lower tripod leg is probably just dirt or wet plaster.

49. "File #946 12/19/15 body of Antonio Pemear (?) Hudson Ave Bklyn murdered in his residence Christensen #529." Something about this tableau is reminiscent of Goya; the figure might be that of an Iberian peasant dead in the Napoleonic wars. The press corrects the impression, revealing the true urban banality of the occasion.

SEES BROTHER SHOT DEAD

Antonio J. Demai, 19 years old, of No. 287 Hudson Street, Brooklyn, was talking to his brother Bernard in front of their home last night when a man stepped up and shot him through the stomach. The boy died in five minutes. The police are searching for a man known to Bernard as Michael Brachi.

[*New York Press*, December 20, 1915]

Here the subject was evidently still alive when laid on the bed. His shoes and hat were hastily pulled off and his clothes opened to get at the wound. Curiously, the pants and underwear were pulled up for the photograph so as to hide the wound, and the only trace of blood is a trickle from the mouth. The murder seems random, although it may have been over money or territory; it is curiously similar to the kind of killings that go on among drug dealers.

50 and **51.** No caption. The setting is a saloon, probably a blind tiger, at basement level. The man is German or Irish, to judge by his complexion; beer and whiskey are the regimen. Cause of death appears to be a head wound, but the chair hides the site of the injury as well as its nature. The discrepancies between the two photographs are puzzling and instructive. The overhead picture was taken before the horizontal one. In the process, the hat has migrated down from the wall to the victim's shoulder, the bottle has rolled from one side of his right leg to the other, and, most peculiarly, the pack of Mecca cigarettes by his right shoulder has been soaked in a new pool of blood, apparently coming from the right side of his face. Other apparent oddities, such as the disappearance of the cards by his right foot, may be explained by the distortion of space effected by the lens (these cards are not, by the way, playing cards, but probably the partial contents of a wallet; one of them is from a firm that might be Lehrman Bros.). Only two of the ten chairs in the room match.

52. No caption. The setting may be a subway or an El station, more probably the latter. The subject would seem to have been attacked through his ticket window and have fallen either while trying to get out or when the police or thieves opened the door. The apparent chalk circle is again caused by damage to the plate. If robbery was the motive, the thieves do not seem to have been interested in the man's watch and chain.

53. "294 Elizabeth St. Domenico Mastropaolos stabbed and slashed to death in wine cellar photo by Golden."

TELEPHONE CALL REVEALS MURDER
Some one telephoned last evening to Dominico Bonomolo, an undertaker at 294 Elizabeth Street, that Dominick Mostropaolo, a wine seller with a shop beneath Bonomolo's place, wanted him. Bonomolo went downstairs and found Mostropaolo dead between two casks, his throat cut. The police of the Elizabeth Street station are trying to find out who telephoned him, and who killed Mostropaolo.
[The New York Times, January 19, 1917]

The variant spellings of the names here (the victim's name was probably Mastropaolo) give an indication of the lack of respect to which Italians were subject at the time.

Headlines routinely featured such wording as "Man attacked by Italians" or "Italian killed in Bronx." Mastropaolo's blood-drenched figure appears to have been dragged, to judge by the dark trail between his legs. The location stood near the north corner of Houston Street and was leveled during the widening of that thoroughfare in the 1950s.

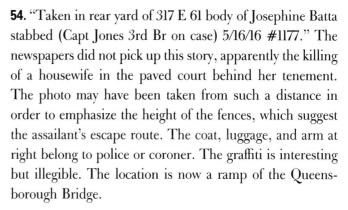

54. "Taken in rear yard of 317 E 61 body of Josephine Batta stabbed (Capt Jones 3rd Br on case) 5/16/16 #1177." The newspapers did not pick up this story, apparently the killing of a housewife in the paved court behind her tenement. The photo may have been taken from such a distance in order to emphasize the height of the fences, which suggest the assailant's escape route. The coat, luggage, and arm at right belong to police or coroner. The graffiti is interesting but illegible. The location is now a ramp of the Queensborough Bridge.

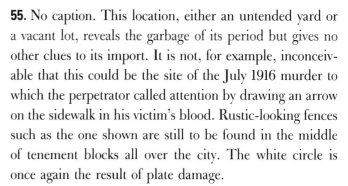

55. No caption. This location, either an untended yard or a vacant lot, reveals the garbage of its period but gives no other clues to its import. It is not, for example, inconceivable that this could be the site of the July 1916 murder to which the perpetrator called attention by drawing an arrow on the sidewalk in his victim's blood. Rustic-looking fences such as the one shown are still to be found in the middle of tenement blocks all over the city. The white circle is once again the result of plate damage.

These cases are steeped in obscurity. All that can be said with any confidence is that they include two murder-suicides (George McAghon and Barbara Cornelius, and Josephine Huntsinger and her children), one crime of passion (the killing of Alberta Thomas), and two fights that led to deaths (those of Helen Wheelan and Giuseppe Certona). The others are either of unknown nature or are dropped unsolved, as they may actually have been in their day. Possibly they include revenge killings, homicides committed during robberies, sex crimes, gang rubouts, union disputes carried out in blood, aggravated manslaughter cases such as meaningless brawls that got out of hand.

The economy of life in New York City, as in the world, fluctuates in cycles. During the period of the pictures, the city was relatively quiet and safe. John Purroy Mitchell was then mayor, the first genuine reformer to have held that office after many years of machine patsies and ineffectual rhetoricians. Among other things, he began a crackdown on gangs, after a gun battle on St. Mark's Place in January 1914 killed a court clerk passing by, and he appears to have succeeded. From 265 homicides in 1913, the number dropped to 244 in 1914, 222 in 1915, 186 in 1916, then rose again to 236 in 1917, going back down to 221 in 1918. The days when whole neighborhoods were shunned for their danger appeared to be gone. The newspapers, all of which were gray and sober in everything but their sports and comics sections (the tabloid era was not to begin until 1919, with the birth of the *Daily News*), did not report much on crime, to a large extent because the popular mind was fixed on other matters: the war in Mexico, the war in Europe, rumors of

German sabotage at the Hoboken docks, the murder by Germans of the heroic British nurse Edith Cavell, the railroading and execution of the legendary IWW leader Joe Hill in Utah. Well before it entered into the Great War, America was gripped with anxiety.

Even so, what went on in the tenements and pool rooms and back alleys was a long way from the world stage. The record of such murders as *The New York Times* found room for in the bottom of its columns speaks of desperation, brutality, and randomness. A father threw his two children out the window; a woman smothered her sister's baby in an apparent fit of jealousy; "in the last six weeks," fourteen infants' bodies were recovered from the East River (the homicide statistics given above specifically exclude infanticides, as well as "abortions, accidental homicides, and justifiable homicides by the police"). People were shot at card games, at dances, after being put out of dances, tossed from taxicabs, beaten to death on Broadway. A hospital orderly was killed by a patient; a patient was slain on his sickbed. A man killed another man for refusing him a cigarette; a boy killed another boy in a feud over a baseball game. An engineer was murdered in the House of Refuge, a shelter on Randall's Island; seven inmates were held. A policeman was beaten to death by a mob. A boy fatally shot another boy while demonstrating Joe Hill's execution by firing squad. People were killed with razors and revolvers and axes, "as a result of a cheek bite," by "a fountain pen driven into the brain," by "an East Indian strangling method," by "acid poured into the mouth by a maniac." Such cases made the papers because they were unusual or lurid, or because there was a column inch or two to fill.

The crime stories that drew the greatest attention were, naturally, those involving the rich, and such things were not rare; "love triangles" figured prominently. None of the people in these photographs occupied that niche, only a couple even qualifying as middle class. Of the traceable stories here, the ones that received the most coverage are the most titillating and the most absurd. Entertainment value was the major criterion for editorial decisions, so that the newspapers that ignored Roshinsky's murder, or Paul Richard's, or those of unnumbered black people, could instead devote space to the man in the gray coat and black hat found wandering in Manhattan, muttering, "Brooklyn, Brooklyn"; or the two transvestites arrested, by a cop who thought they were women, for "immodestly raising their skirts." Heroin overdoses, too, made the papers, because they were still rare, as well as abductions, because they seemed glamorous, and raids on gambling dens, because the district attorney wanted the publicity. If the value of life was then, to judge by the homicide figures, higher than it had been previously or has become since, it was nevertheless not a thing of reverence.

The pictures here can be said to represent a cross section of what murder and its locales looked like at the time. Their selection was decided by several quasi-random processes: by the police, who did not photograph every crime scene; by the preservation or lack thereof of the photos themselves; and by my own culling, which was entirely aesthetic, while not, I think, favoring any one kind of tableau, although I omitted the pictures that I could not stomach, such as those involving advanced decomposition. The archive includes no pictures of rich victims, or dead babies, or dead cops. Beyond this, few generalizations can be made. The victims are male and female, old and young, black and white, fat and thin, respectable and (probably) criminal. The disproportionate representation of Italians may be in part accounted for by the fact that their gangs and disputes were then nearly as impenetrable to the police (who were still overwhelmingly Irish, with Germans as the most visible minority) as those of the Chinese and Vietnamese are today. While Mitchell's crackdown had affected the Jewish and remaining Irish gangs, sending hundreds of men to jail or into hiding in other states, the Mafia and Camorra continued their feuds and vendettas largely outside the normal spheres of police surveillance. The case of Gaspare Candella, found in a barrel in a Sunset Park lot, is almost certainly the result of one of these; the corpse in plate 3, who has not been robbed, who is well dressed despite evidence of a hard life, and whose head lies about six inches from a crumpled copy of a New York Italian newspaper, is perhaps another.

What is most striking in these pictures to the present-day eye is the discrepancy between the respectable façades that people maintained and the horribly constrained conditions of their lives. Nearly all the male victims are dressed in collar and tie (or those accoutrements, removed in the search for wounds, are lying nearby). Dark three-piece suits predominate. In life they would all have worn hats. The women tolerated assemblages of underwear that would require hours of laborious laundering, and their hair, uncut and pinned, would demand constant home care. Their rooms, often tiny, are equally dressed, with complex figured wallpaper (cheaper than painting, in those days) and often threadbare but ornate carpets, sometimes laid over equally complex linoleum patterns, and sometimes curtains, flounces, runners, doilies. There are ancestral portraits and knickknacks, pennants and framed prints. Calendars sometimes appear in multiples, more for their decorative value than for their usefulness. The imagery runs to beauties in large hats, pastoral scenes, and patriotic motifs. The young black man in plate 47 has been particularly ambitious in his decorating: fabric patches of flags line the shelves, each series bearing the Stars and Stripes in its center; the right-hand wall features a montage of scenes from a play or possibly a movie, probably a discard from a theater. Every bit of wall space bears an image. Tucked into the top of a giveaway calendar near the right-hand margin are two studio group photographs, all of white people. Were these friends, or just pictures he acquired? Was the room possibly not his own, but just the room he died in? The people who lived in tenements, who had to fit their beds around a stove and a table, were cramped but relatively autonomous, with control of their own heat and cooking.

Others lived in hall bedrooms only big enough for a twin mattress and the smallest available chest of drawers. The spaces are virtually all still lit by gas, nearly four decades after the development of the incandescent bulb. Hardly any would have had toilets, these being located in the hall; baths, needless to say, would have been absent altogether. The rooms are tidy or untidy; a few are clean, but most, in a time of overdressed furnishings and before the vacuum cleaner, are not, just as the streets are not. The accumulation of garbage nearly everywhere is distinguished from that of our own day only by the absence of plastic and its analogues.

The occupations we find among the recorded cases are: assistant railroad yardmaster, oysterman, lodging-house keeper, cabaret singer, private detective, chauffeur, process server, plasterer, contractor, undertaker, wine seller, "railroad man," and something in connection with a produce house at a market. Since nearly all these are service professions, the demographics of the period would require that many of the unidentified have had positions in factories, or, for that matter, on the docks or in stables. The faces are mostly beyond our reckoning. Just try to put an age to any of them. Life lines ran shorter then, with an average term of expectancy that did not hit sixty summers, and people consequently were fixed at twenty, seamed at thirty, sagging at forty, depleted at fifty. Diets were poor: people ate beans and organ meats and cabbage boiled until it had the consistency of wet tissue paper. Upton Sinclair's *The Jungle*, published in 1906, may have

inspired the passing of the Pure Food and Drug Act, but blue milk and parasite-infected meat and bread dough eked out with sawdust and worthless if not outright perilous patent medicines were not yet obsolete in the lives of the poor. People died of tuberculosis and assorted other lung ailments, of complications from childbirth, of syphilis, of gout, of "chronic indigestion," of "nervous disorders," and, in great numbers, from the Spanish influenza. It was the twentieth century, with all its perils and discoveries coming one atop the other, but most of the people pictured would have seen the nineteenth. The man in plate 44 may have been a Civil War veteran; Pasquale Caruso, who fought under Garibaldi in the sixties, was born around 1836, when rural Italy was still medieval. Few of these people would have ever ridden in an automobile, or had occasion to use a telephone, or heard a gramophone outside a department store.

But the faces also say, "Et in Arcadia ego." We cannot know what trails led them to the bedrooms and vacant lots and barroom floors where they met death. Which of the young women, of plate 8 or plate 36 or those whose faces are hidden, began life in pleasant rustic monotony and chased their ambitions to the metropolis, like Sister Carrie Meeber but without her cunning? Was the corpulent man in plate 29 a happy paterfamilias who happened to find himself backed into a skin game in an unfamiliar saloon and then protested the outcome? Was John Rogers a deacon on his way to services who was ambushed in his foyer by an apprentice triggerman demonstrating his mettle? Was he born of former slaves in the South, or of a line of Northern freemen? Was he forced to bow before white people all day long, allowed to arise in the evening to strut among his own? Was the bartender in plate 11 an Elk or a Red Man, and did he have the inside wire on prizefights or elections, and was he killed because he picked the wrong horse? Was the man in plate 27 saving money toward a small farm in south Jersey when he stepped into a quarrel between the husband and wife next door? Was the unfortunate in plate 45 somebody's useless cousin who was given a night watchman's job to keep him eating, and seemed to be acquiring stability of character in the process, when he bought it in the course of a hijack by a rival wholesale grocer? Was Marion Hart a runaway wife from a brutal Moravian settlement in western Pennsylvania who had found peace and anonymity in a squatter's shack in the obscure middle of Staten Island? Was she killed for love or money or in a mindless drunken frenzy? Was the youth in plate 20 a smooth ladies' man with a swift line of patter who finally got his from one of a series of enraged husbands? Was the character in plate 34 a successful immigrant entrepreneur with a horizon of spiraling lucrative deals who was signposted as a warning to others of his kind to take seriously the need for protection payments to the local brotherhood of wise ones? Were the men in plate 40 shop steward and treasurer of an affiliate of the Fur Trimmers or the Hat Blockers or the Paperhangers who were blackjacked and kicked eight flights into space

on orders from a fat cider-drinking fancier of military marches as he sat on a towel in the steam room of a Sixth Avenue bathhouse? What had they all done the day before? How many were born on farms? Which of them could swim, or play music, or divine the age of a horse at a glance, or do fast mental arithmetic, or tell good jokes? How many were in love? How many had been?

Outside, a crowd gathered as the body was carried to the Black Maria, people craning their necks to get a view of the hidden face, small children scared and excited, a few acquaintances crying softly, others cornering the landlady to make a deal for the furniture or the clothes or unbloodied bedding. The crowd might be stunned for a few hours or a few days, and imagine that whoever had hit Shorty or Elsie might come after them, and walk with greater care and hang a ladderback chair from the doorknob at night, but before long they would forget about the incident except possibly as a place-marker in their historical memory, so that they would come to refer to "the winter that Willie Murphy across the street was killed." The bodies would be taken to the undertaker's and then to church or synagogue and eventually to one of the patchwork of ethnic graveyards in the vast cemetery tracts of central Queens, or perhaps from the morgue to a boat to a mass trench on Hart's Island in Long Island Sound. Widows and widowers might remarry or continue to pine, and perhaps in an occasional case or two there might actually be an estate and a will to contest. Such survivors or descendants as might exist would perhaps move to the suburbs, to farm country, to California, maybe changing their names and even their histories along the way, eventually to found a line of succession of fully assimilated Americans with automatic garage-door openers and tennis-club memberships and unacknowledged chemical dependencies.

In the streets of New York, meanwhile, the tenements would sag, maybe collapse, maybe be razed to make way for housing projects, and the pavements would buckle and at length be replaced, and the vacant lots would be paved over and built upon, and the saloons would be shuttered in just a few years' time, after which their locations would be occupied by haberdashers and their proprietors would remove to one flight upstairs or down or to a barely concealed back room. The contrast would be maintained between the surging crowds of daytime midtown and the lunar vacancy of night in warehouse districts. People would continue to be killed, in greater numbers through the 1920s and early thirties, then falling, and falling further, at least in New York City, through the forties, then rising again, slowly at first, and then rapidly and more rapidly up to the present. The police would find and print and tag and photograph and cover with sheets an unending parade of supine figures in hallways and bars and salt marshes and parked cars. The graves of the dead here pictured might be obliterated by weeds, while the pictures themselves would slowly settle, the ones in the backs of the drawers eventually giving way and cracking under the weight of the slanted pile, in a basement on Centre Street, their case records meanwhile being lost over time to floods and decay in another basement a quarter-mile or so down the same thoroughfare, the names and incidents gone from all memory. Before long, it would be as if they had never existed at all.

The first instance of evidentiary photography in the literature comes early. In November 1839, only two years after Daguerre had refined Niepce's earlier invention and coined his own term for the result, newspapers in France made mention of a case in which a husband had allegedly obtained evidence of his wife's infidelity via daguerreotype. Given the lighting and the exposure time required for the process then, the story sounds like myth. Two years after that, however, more substantial reports were made of the Parisian police photographing habitual criminals. Rogues' galleries were soon adopted by all major police departments: New York by 1858, Danzig in 1864, Moscow in 1867, London in 1870. Paris, ever the pioneer, had a full police photo laboratory in place by 1874. The first mentions of crime-scene photography come from Switzerland around 1860; the first instance of an eviden-

tiary photograph invalidating an eyewitness account in a court of law apparently dates from 1867, location unknown.

The reasons for photographing scenes of crime appear not to have been immediately evident. For some years, in fact, the use of evidentiary photography was tangled in both official and popular minds with an old superstition: that the retina of the eye retains after death the imprint of the last image it has seen. Therefore, it was thought, if the eyes of a murder victim were photographed, the face of his or her assassin would appear within the image of the pupil. A London photographer, William H. Warner, claimed in the 1860s to have taken a picture of the eye of a dead calf, and to have found within it the image of lines, which were, he claimed, the boards of the slaughterhouse floor. The idea caught the imagination of the world. Newspapers published accounts of successful applications, always in faraway locations; the method turned up in the denouements of numerous detective stories. A professor at the University of Heidelberg spent many years solemnly beheading rabbits and fixing their retinas in alum to halt the sensitization of the membrane, which, it had been established by then, continued after death. The idea would not go away, even after it had been disproved and ridiculed in medical journals. Its application was urged during the Jack the Ripper killings, and as late as 1925, and possibly 1948, police scientists were still struggling with it in various countries.

Gradually, though, the bona-fide grounds for the use of on-site photography crept in. Charles C. Scott, who in 1942 wrote the first comprehensive manual for the courtroom use of photographic evidence in the United States (I searched for the earliest available works on forensic photography; none of the American ones predated 1935), compiled a succinct list of the basic reasons: to prove that the crime was committed in the county or municipality where the body was found and the trial scheduled; to give proof of the corpus delicti (i.e., the corpse, as well as the actual fact of the crime) and its venue; to help establish a motive, by means, for example, of the position of the body; to refute any imputation of suicide; and to clarify the relationship of the body to the weapon and any other properties. Outside the courtroom, photographic evidence might help identify the unknown dead, or help establish a similarity of method to other unsolved crimes, or detect even more subtle proofs. Harry Söderman and John J. O'Connell cite the following in their popular-science work, *Modern Criminal Investigation* (1935):

In Vienna, some years ago, a young woman sitting on a bench in a public park was found dead. She had apparently shot herself through the head with a pistol which was lying in a natural position where it had presumably slipped from her hand. The scene was immediately photographed—in the early morning before sunrise. Later in the day, after developing the plate, the police photographer discovered that a person had been sitting close to the woman. This was shown by the marks in the dew which had collected on the bench. The marks were very faint, but the photographic lens had caught them before evaporation had taken place. Investigation brought out the fact that a homicide had been committed.

This immediately takes us back to Benjamin—"Does not the photographer . . . uncover guilt in his pictures?" The cold eye of the camera records things that the frail and emotional human eye cannot see.

When I first came across these pictures, I thought that they were the work of a single artist, and that their similarities constituted a style. Looking at the surviving captions, at first barely comprehensible, I eventually realized that some of them included attributions, that at least six separate photographers were involved, and that what was at stake was not so much a style as a method, the consequence both of available equipment and of departmental rules, probably improvised and gradually refined over the years, about the proper coverage of crime scenes. Plates 4, 43, and 49 are by "Christensen"; 7, 18, 19, 39, and 53 by "Golden"; 13 and 37 by "Z"; 47 by "DeVoe"; 15 by "Chas. Abrams"; and 30 by "Charles E. Carsbrer." I had thought these might be civilian photographers hired by the police department, until John Podracky of the Police Museum told me that the pictures had always been taken by detectives. Denied access to NYPD records, I consulted the *Civil List*, the annual register of all civil servants, for the relevant years. This told me that in 1915 John A. Golden, Clement A. Christensen, and Arthur W. DeVoe were all acting detective sergeants, second grade, in the Detective Bureau's Special Squad Number Five. The following year, they and about ten others came under the rubric of the Bureau of Criminal Identification. The "Z," I guessed, was most likely Frederick F. E. Zwirz, the only man in either of those groupings possessing that initial; having two of that letter in his name would guarantee him the moniker. In 1917, Golden and Zwirz were made full detective sergeants, while Christensen and DeVoe were knocked back down to patrolman status. I found nothing at all on Abrams or Carsbrer; since they alone used both barrels of their names, they may indeed have been outsiders, possibly civilian specialists hired in exceptional circumstances when no trained detectives were available.

Golden and Zwirz were the only ones to have left traces in the form of obituaries. Golden died in 1941 at the age of fifty-six, after a long illness, nearly five years after his retirement as a captain and as commander of the East Twenty-second Street station. He had spent just under thirty years on the force, joining it in 1907 and becoming a lieutenant in 1922. His specialty was identification, and he had toured Europe to study fingerprinting and other modern methods. He became head of the Bureau of Criminal Identification in 1925. He raised some controversy when, after a trip to Bermuda, he came forward to advocate public flogging, which he had seen practiced on that island. He remained his whole career an advocate of universal fingerprinting. He never married. Zwirz died in 1962, aged eighty-five. He had joined the force in 1901 and retired in 1946. He was likewise an identification specialist, having been the first man in the department to learn the fingerprinting method from the future Deputy Police Commissioner Joseph A. Faurot, who in turn had acquired the science at Scotland Yard. Zwirz was for many years head of the fingerprinting division of the Criminal Identification Bureau, and in that capacity worked on the Lindbergh kidnap case and the $427,000 Rubel Ice Company hold-up in Brooklyn. He, too, appears never to have married.

These identifications are unproven, but seem more than plausible. Crime-scene photography would likely have been the province of the same group of policemen who handled fingerprinting, at least at that time, when the latter art was a comparative novelty. Much less is known about how the photographers worked. The police *Annual Reports*, the principal public documents issued by the department as a source of general information, make no mention whatsoever of photography until decades later. There are stray mentions in legal literature of New York City cases affected by the introduction into evidence of crime-scene photographs going back as far as the 1880s, but there is no indication that these were taken by the police. Systematic use, which began in some European countries in the 1860s, may not have begun in New York until much later. The photographs in the archive are numbered chronologically, the earliest, from 1914, carrying figures in the 500s; the latest, from 1918, approaching 2000. Even allowing for an increase over the years in the number of pictures taken, this does not suggest that number 1 would far predate 1910.

The photographers' equipment is unknown. John Podracky believes the main camera, in those days before the Speed Graphic and the Graphlex, was something called a Bird's Eye, and that the wide-angle lens of unusual caliber (approximately 25 mm., bordering on fish-eye) was probably custom-made for the NYPD. Certainly they would have used magnesium powder, with sulphur as a reagent, which produced such a blinding flash that it temporarily immobilized those caught by it (and so allowed Jacob Riis, for example, despite his cumbersome equipment, to take a surprise photo in a stale-beer dive and make a clean getaway). Podracky cites an old police

cameraman to the effect that nighttime outdoor shots were taken by pulling a coat over one's head, leaving the lens open, and firing off the flash every ten paces, meanwhile changing the plates. The tripods were presumably equipped with ball-socket joints and a pivoting plate, but even so, considerable labor must have been expended in the process of changing the apparatus from a horizontal to an overhead trajectory. In all probability, only one camera was used by the department for these purposes during this time, when crime-scene photography was not done every day, or even necessarily every week. That six or more photographers were involved can only reflect the rotation of their other chores.

What I mistook for a style, a signature, proved to be the result of elements that do not admit a notion of style. But this style, or pseudo-style, is so unique and strong that, idly leafing through yet another popularized introduction to scientific crime-busting (*Camera! Take the Stand*, by Asa S. Herzog and A. J. Ezickson, 1940), I was immediately riveted by two postage-stamp-sized reproductions of "actual crime photos used in cases by the New York police." The pictures, too small to make out in detail, were nevertheless obviously from the same body of work as the pictures herein: same camera, same lighting, same lens, probably the same general time-frame (their shattered plates may now be lying off Corlear's Hook). Somehow I had known this before peering closely at them or even reading the caption. There is no getting around the fact that these pictures look different from other pictures of their time, of their kind, or even of their kind at their time; art photographers in 1915 were pursuing other goals, other police photographers then (judging from the small amount of such work that has been published) employed other methods. Their "style" is only the result of conditions combined to cram the maximum amount of information into the frame: the most inclusive lens short of hallucinatory distortion, the most intense lighting, the most comprehensive framing and coverage of the subject. In addition, naturally, various random factors of choice and availability are introduced into the equation. The light, the lens, and the fairly lengthy exposure time required by the lens and the plate, make for an elliptical penumbra that darkens to black at the borders, giving the pictures their singular glow. It is an effect that persists even in the outdoor daylight shots. This glow isolates the central figures and wraps them in stillness. In the overhead shots, it almost makes them levitate. The glow conveys a softness that might almost be mistaken for sympathy, or even lyricism, if we see the pictures without knowing their context. That is why these pictures do not resemble the brutal corpse shots that used to be found in tabloids, why certain critics, if they could get beyond the fact that they show dead people, might call them "humanist." They slug the eye and caress it in the same gesture. Yet these effects are merely technical results. Does that subvert their existence or deny their value?

A number of other questions await, all of which cluster around one that is unanswerable: To what use were these pictures meant to be put? There are numerous compelling reasons for photographing the scene of a crime, and the precepts behind the method on view—inclusion, illumination, coverage—cannot be gainsaid. Such being the case, then why have the weapons been removed? Why have the bodies been tampered with before photography? Why have such essentials as the body and the objects surrounding and touching it been shifted between one view and the next (plates 50 and 51)? Why has furniture apparently been taken out of the way (plate 31)? Why have apparently pointless scenes been included (plates 7, 24, 42, 43)? Why is the coverage so erratic? The last question falls outside the bounds of this inquiry and in fact cannot be answered. The archive, while containing exhaustive series of shots of certain scenes, also contains single, sometimes remote views of incidents that demand full coverage—the missing pictures may once have existed, but no longer do. The apparently pointless pictures may answer to an agenda we can no longer divine: the empty landscapes may illustrate the position of a wall or a window, or the direction of light at a given time, or the condition of the ground. A picture of a dead dog (plate 33) would seem to have little bearing on criminal matters—it would be in the province of the ASPCA or civil litigation—but its position may shed light on that of a nearby human body, for example. The case of the Panther Boys fray (plate 7) appears the hardest to justify, since we seem to have the basic and unimpressive facts, but the size of the room or the position of its exits may have been significant. Anyway, the policeman's predilections for pomp and gadgetry, even when inappropriate, should not be discounted, either.

The other questions all pertain to alterations of the scene before photography. The simplest answer is probably that the flatfoots, not always informed of the latest scientific methods, got to the scene an hour or more before the downtown boys could make it, and fulfilled what they saw as their duty, leaving the photographer to make the best of a bad situation. Cornelius Cahane's *Police Practice and Procedure*, published in 1914 and, as its title page boasts, "distributed free of charge to every member of the New York Police Department," gives the basic drill for cops arriving at the scene of a violent crime. They are to discharge all firearms, while taking care not to wipe off any prints, and the latter goes for knives as well. Of the dying or wounded they are to ask, after getting a name and address:

"Do you believe that you are about to die from the effects of the injury you have received?"

and

"Are you willing to make a true statement of how and in what manner you received the injury from which you are now suffering?"

(One can imagine the response this sort of verbiage would provoke from recent immigrants in extremis.) In the case of a homicide, tags with the date and the names of the deceased and the suspect are to be attached to each item of clothing. Medical aid can be summoned with a blow of the whistle or by yelling out the window. The book does, however, instruct the cop:

Permit no one to touch or handle any weapon or furniture which might contain finger impressions of the assailant. If there is evidence of a struggle, such as furniture or bedding disturbed or blood-stained, do not disturb it.

After the beat cops would come any nearby ranking officers, who would do their own poking around for clues, and then the body would have to be fingerprinted, and the man in charge of this might leave with all objects potentially handled by the assailant. If the victim was not dead when the beat cops came in, they would have looked for the wound, and the first available doctor would have as well, and then the coroner would search the body after death. Since the room would by this time be crawling with people, and the photographer would be the only one of them who required a clear field for his work, his turn would probably come last. When it came, he might have to move this chair and that bucket in order to properly dispose the legs of his tripod. After all this, the room would bear little resemblance to its original condition.

What use such epistemologically flawed photographs could have for legal or investigative purposes is open to question. Scott in his book stresses that, in court, testimony would be required that the body was undisturbed at the time of photography. "However," he continues, "even though the position of the body was disturbed before the photograph was taken, the picture is admissible if any discrepancy caused by medical examination and handling is adequately explained." He says nothing about the removal of major props or weapons, perhaps assuming such a thing unthinkable. L. A. Waters, writing on the subject in *American Photography*, March 1937, is strict about method, recommending two shots from overhead at opposing 45° angles, additional shots from or near ground level to reveal anything possibly concealed by the corpse without altering its position, as well as shots from all four corners of the room after the body has been removed. "In this type of work the lighting should be full and complete," he goes on. "This is unlike other types of photography, in that no attempt is made to secure an artistic result."

Somehow these photographs were supposed to represent the truth, some of the truth, some kind of truth. They gave witness that something had happened, in a room or a field, that a person or persons had existed, and no longer did, that the remains of such persons exhibited signs of violence, or the lack thereof. The violence had occurred in the place depicted or outside of it, at a time of day or night proximate to or remote from the time shown, by means imaginable or unimaginable from the depiction. There is no idea of what evidence might have been sought from these pictures that can be proposed without an exception immediately coming to hand among these fifty-five examples. Only that something happened, and that the occurrence left behind a body, a relic, or a site.

Their function, therefore, must have been literally as souvenirs, memory aids, records for records' sake. They probably served as markers for reference, tools for training novice homicide detectives, minor props accessory to the work of fingerprint analysis, questioning of suspects, and milking of informers that would dredge up the answers if the answers were there to be dredged. They may have been employed for their shock value during interrogations, when the bad cop of the Mutt-and-Jeff team would find a critical moment to spring it on the suspect, who would exhibit horror or fear or glee or indifference, or possibly break down and admit to everything between choked sobs.

When the cases they illustrated had been declared closed, they were put away, herded into cabinets and the drawers shut, and then they were, in all probability, forgotten. For decades they lay inert, in hiding. Now,

through a succession of chance occurrences, we are looking at them. Only a few threads of documentation survive
to connect us with the hours and days that surrounded
these moments, or with the ground that lay just outside
their margins. We are given exceptional access to one
remote instant in one spot, as if we were allowed to look
at the past through a keyhole. We have the illusion that
we are spared any interpretation of the view, that the lens
is neutral, that we are permitted to choose our own stance,
proportion, and moral. The pictures are silent, or are
pools of silence within a commotion discernible only at
their borders. They are dream images.

Through the act of looking, we own these pictures, or,
rather, they thrust themselves upon us. Their private cool
centers can seduce us, even as we are repelled by the
signs of violent death. We may feel that we know them,
that they are familiar from some anterior existence, as
perhaps they are. We are absolutely alone with them, one
at a time, and the darkness that beckons outside the circle
of flash might be a cosmos, or the cosmos, in which the
dead are radiant and we are shadowed. Theirs is a fin-
ished story, aglow at its instant of closure; ours remains
ambiguous and indeterminate, fortunately for us. To look
at these pictures is to glimpse the work of the recording
angel on the day of judgment, knowing that the whole
vast tide of humanity is composed of myriad individual
destinies each of which terminates in such a scene, a
body sprawled on a bed or a floor or the dirt, eyes staring
or shut, no more to be written, the last card played. The
unimportance of these subjects matches our own unimportance, which should help us to recognize our affinity
with them, although fear prevents us from full identification. Such a likeness is the one photograph of ourselves
we are certain never to see.

Here we are on the other side of the camera, in the
position of the disinterested photographer, who by choosing one view precludes alternatives. But in these pictures
where nothing can move by its own agency, the scene as
fixed permits no variation, regardless of intention. When
associated with the manifestation of law in the flesh of
the police, the photograph threatens to make itself iden-
tical with a larger truth: *Everyone dies* (but we know that);
Everyone is humbled by death (perhaps); *Everyone dies in
misery, from the machinations of evil* (do we trust this?).
The police photographer inevitably portrays life in terms
of its negation, and furthermore cannot help emphasizing
the unseen presence of malign force. The aureola of light
surrounding the victim is contrasted with the peripheral
darkness: the corpse is incapable of transgression, but
the world outside is a forest of dangers. Is this why we
can find these pictures beautiful, because their subjects,
having exited life, are finally in a state of grace?

Every photograph is a regret; it is an end. There is no
sequel to what it depicts, no means of expanding it. This
portrait, that street scene, that crowd—all are suspended.
Their fixedness tantalizes: we want them to hold that
pose, because it is so beautiful or instructive, and we also
want (maybe secretly, maybe it seems vulgar) to see the

next frame, to follow up on what we contrive as the story (we insist on finding stories everywhere). These photographs of cadavers rob us even of speculation, since what they show can only be succeeded by decay. Flailing about for some kind of satisfaction, we invent a religion for them—in the incidental effects of the photographic process we imagine we can see halos, just as we are wont to confuse the eye of the police with the eye of God. The reason for this is terror. These pictures are documentary evidence of an end we are afraid to recognize.

Among these photographs are some representations of the void, an undefined lack of mass temporarily situated near a lot or a park or a road. The others contain bodies, some observed from a small distance horizontally, others from directly overhead and caged by the insect's carapace of the tripod legs, as well as clues and artifacts, clothing and garbage, printed matter and bric-a-brac. They are tombs, like the pyramids outfitting the corpse with the effects of its life. Each, as well, might be the last photograph, the full stop toward which all photography inexorably draws, the pinned specimen of an extinguished race, the monument to the Unknown Human. As we look at them the clocks have all stopped, the air is going out of the world, the great glass bell is descending on the circumference. There is no place for us outside the frame, nothing to breathe, nowhere to stand. We cannot be the viewer of such a scene. We must have forgotten: We are the subject.